The LEFT BEHIND *Deception*

REVEALING DANGEROUS ERRORS ABOUT
THE RAPTURE AND THE ANTICHRIST

Steve Wohlberg

ISBN 1–883012–90–2

Published by
Remnant Publications
649 E. Chicago
Coldwater, MI 43096

Credits
Cover Design — Gary Will
Editing, Typesetting — Robert Bethel

*All Bible verses taken from the King James Version
unless otherwise noted.*

Table of Contents

Acknowledgments

I cannot possibly thank everyone who has contributed to this special project, yet there are a few who most recently stand out in my mind — Leighton Holley for his continual backbone support of my ministry; Costin Jordache and Art Humphrey for their friendship and insights; Pat Jones for her voluntary editorial assistance with this manuscript; all of my friends at the *Texas Media Center*; Gary Will for his time and graphic abilities; Robert Bethel for his much needed help in preparing this book for the press; my father, Gene Wohlberg, for his encouragement and constant interest; my beautiful wife Kristin, for her love, patience, suggestions, and support during the many hours involved in writing this book.

Above all, I want to thank Jesus Christ, my Savior, who suffered, bled and died to save me by His grace.

Author's Introduction

On radio, television, the World Wide Web, and in countless other places, Christians are now talking about a best-selling book called *Left Behind,* which is all about Bible prophecy, the rise of the Antichrist, and the end of the world. It all began in 1995 when *Left Behind* first hit Christian bookstores nationwide. The authors, Bible scholar Tim LaHaye and writer Jerry Jenkins, scarcely dreamed that Barnes & Noble would eventually call *Left Behind* "one of the top ten best-selling books of the 20th century." Because of soaring sales and blockbuster success, the authors decided to expand their project into a sequence of twelve books. Amazingly, these books have recently rocketed onto the best-seller lists of the *New York Times,* the *Wall Street Journal*, and *USA Today,* and have resulted in an interview of LaHaye and Jenkins on *Larry King Live*. The novels have even been labeled "...the most successful Christian fiction series ever" — *Publishers Weekly.* On February 2, 2001, in the wake of a truly massive advertising campaign, *LEFT*

BEHIND: The Movie opened in theaters all over the United States.

The primary writer, Jerry Jenkins, is a master storyteller. His *Left Behind* books are fictitious novels which present a fascinating portrayal of what many believe might actually occur during "Earth's last days" when Biblical prophecies described in the book of Revelation are finally fulfilled.

The *Left Behind* novels begin with the sudden vanishing of millions of Christians into thin air (an event called the Rapture). The rest of mankind, having been left behind, suddenly wake up to the nightmare of a world gone mad. Driverless cars crash, pilotless planes collide, and universal panic sweeps over the globe as a final apocalyptic period called "the Tribulation" is ushered in. In the midst of unimaginable chaos, the mysterious Nicolae Carpathia, representing the Antichrist, rises to world leadership with promises of peace. Carpathia takes control of the United Nations and quickly establishes a one-world government. Yet not everyone follows this end-time seducer. A group of new Christians, calling themselves the Tribulation Force, see through Nicolae's disguise and determine to resist his hypnotic power. Finally, in a last ditch attempt to gain total control of the world, Carpathia unveils his ultimate test of loyalty — the insertion of a high-tech biochip (called the Mark of the Beast) into the foreheads and hands of all people.

Truly, *"Left Behind* is overflowing with suspense, action and adventure" (quote from the video cover of *LEFT BEHIND: The Movie*). In both the books and the movie, the drama follows the lives of certain people who, having missed the Rapture, are forced to struggle against the Antichrist and his deadly Mark. Just as millions of Americans are now following the lives of their favorite soap opera actors and actresses, even so are millions of Christians now following the fictitious lives of Rayford Steele, Buck Williams, Hattie Durham, Dr. Chaim Rosenzweig, and Nicolae Carpathia as the *Left Behind* saga continues to unfold.

While *Left Behind* is quite imaginative, its hidden power lies in the belief that underneath the fiction lies the rock bottom fact of Bible truth. Comments like these could be multiplied: "*LEFT BEHIND: The Movie* is an excellent portrayal of what the Bible declares will actually happen following the rapture" (Dr. Bill Bright, President, *Campus Crusade for Christ*). "The main features of this story are not fiction. Those not prepared will be left behind" (Dr. John F. Walvoord, Dallas). "This film is sensitively written, beautifully directed, acted, and produced. I feel it's certainly one of the very best Christian-produced films ever made…" (Pat Boone, *Actor*).

Authors LaHaye and Jenkins sincerely hope to impress their readers to choose Jesus Christ immediately so they can go to heaven in the Rapture, escape the Tribulation, and thus avoid having to face the Antichrist and the Mark. There is no doubt that millions of hearts are being touched by this project, that people are being influenced to give their lives to Jesus Christ, and that Christians everywhere are being led to think more seriously about the final days and the coming of the Lord. Even young people are being affected through a special version of *Left Behind* books just for kids, which includes a Tribulation Force Underground Kit.

Although the producers of *Left Behind* are sincere Christians, nevertheless, we believe it is important to ask these serious questions: Underneath the excitement of this incredibly popular story, is it possible that something is *just not quite right?* Could it be that in the midst of *Left Behind's* focus on missing people, major Bible truths are also missing? Even worse, could an unimaginable cloud of deception be settling over the Christian world? The purpose of this book is to take a closer look at what God's Word says about the Rapture and the Antichrist. We want to find out whether any significant *Bible truth has been left behind*.

Chapter 1
The Rapture — Is Anything Missing?

An official *Left Behind* site on the Internet declares: "In one chaotic moment, millions of people around the world suddenly disappear leaving their clothes, wedding rings, eye glasses and shoes in crumpled piles. Mass confusion hits while vehicles suddenly unmanned veer out of control, fires erupt and hysteria breaks out as the living stare in disbelief and fear at the empty places where their loved ones were just seconds before. This is the rapture that God has planned as the first sign to begin the unraveling of the end of time."

Newspaper headlines are predicted to read: "Millions Mysteriously Vanish!" "All Children Have Disappeared!" "Massive Traffic Snarls Due to Missing Drivers!" "Planes Crash, Trains Wreck As Pilots and Engineers Disappear!" It has been reported that some at American Airlines are worried about this, so they want at least one non-Christian pilot aboard each flight — just in case!

The Bible certainly does teach the exciting truth that Jesus Christ will return for His people. Jesus Himself said, "I will come again, and receive you to myself" (John 14:3). I fully believe these words, and long to be ready for that great day.

Without a doubt, the most quoted passage in the Bible now being used to support the idea of a Rapture is found in 1 Thessalonians 4:17. Countless Christians know it by heart, and it is cited in *LEFT BEHIND: The Movie.* Paul wrote that believers in Jesus Christ will someday be "caught up…in the clouds, to meet the Lord in the air" (1 Thessalonians 4:17). How wonderful! This will be no imaginary, "Beam me up, Scotty," event as in the television series *Star Trek.* On the contrary, it will be very real, and no space suits or oxygen masks will be needed. While I do believe in the return of Jesus, and that believers will someday be "caught up," there are still some major issues of interpretation I want to examine. The first concerns *the timing* of our being "caught up," and the second has to do with *the nature* of the event itself.

Let me explain. According to *Left Behind,* the return of Jesus Christ actually takes place in two distinct phases. First, Jesus returns silently and secretly, unnoticed by the world. At that moment Christians will be "caught up," or raptured, which is interpreted as the *sudden vanishing* of millions of people all over the globe. The rest of mankind, having been left behind, are then ushered into a "seven-year period called the Tribulation" (*The Tribulation Force,* inside cover, second book in the *Left Behind* series). During the Tribulation, the Antichrist rises to enforce his deadly mark. At the end of the seven years, Jesus returns visibly before the eyes of all, an event referred to as Christ's Second Coming or "Glorious Appearing." Thus, according to *Left Behind,* Jesus first comes silently to rapture away true believers, and then, seven years later, He comes visibly at the very end of the world. With minor variations, this sequence is now accepted by millions of Bible-believing Christians as an accurate picture of end-time events.

There are three primary pillars that stand out in this teaching, and it is safe to say that the entire *Left Behind* house rests firmly on top of each of them.

Pillar 1 – The Rapture, when the Church is "caught up" (1 Thessalonians 4:17), does *not* take place at the visible Second Coming of Jesus Christ, but seven years before it.

Pillar 2 – Those who miss the Rapture will have a *second chance* during the seven years of Tribulation to be saved.

Pillar 3 – The true Church of today will *escape the Tribulation* and will *not* have to face the Antichrist and the Mark.

Before we go any further, allow me to list three logical alternatives, thus clarifying the issues.

Alternative 1 – The Rapture, when the Church is "caught up" (1 Thessalonians 4:17), *does* take place at the visible Second Coming of Jesus Christ at the end of world.

Alternative 2 – Those who are not ready for the catching up of true believers at the Second Coming of Jesus Christ will have *no second chance* to be saved.

Alternative 3 – The Church of today will *go through* Earth's final period of Tribulation and therefore must overcome the Antichrist and the Mark in order to be ready for Christ's Second Coming.

Can you see how serious these issues are? Which view is right — The three pillars of *Left Behind,* or these three logical alternatives? *What does the Bible really say?*

Let's start with Pillar 1 — The Rapture does *not* take place at the Second Coming of Jesus Christ. As I have already mentioned, the most widely quoted passage about the Rapture is found in 1 Thessalonians 4:17. There Paul wrote, "We which are alive and remain shall be caught up." Although the word "rapture" doesn't appear anywhere in the Bible, the idea comes from those two words "caught up." A simple comparison of verse 17 with verse 15, which says, "We which are alive and remain to the coming of the Lord," makes it very clear that believers will be "caught up" at "the coming of the Lord." Here is the key issue — *At which coming of the Lord?* Will believers be caught up at a silent and invisible coming of the Lord, before the Tribulation, as taught in *Left Behind* or will believers be caught up at the highly visible "Glorious Appearing" of Jesus Christ at the end of the world? Before we read the entire context, it is important to realize that Paul uses a very specific Greek word for "coming" in verse 15. The word is "parousia," which you can find in any concordance. You may find this a little hard to believe, but a whole lot rides on that one word. If you are a high-tech person, click "Save," and store that word in your mental computer, for we will come back to it.

Have you ever driven down a highway without realizing how fast you were going, and then, when you finally looked down at your speedometer, you said to yourself, "I'm going too fast and must slow down!"? This is what we need to do when it comes to our study of 1 Thessalonians 4. We must slow down and take a full look. As we do, we will discover truth that is not only clear, but also shocking. In fact, the implications are nothing short of cataclysmic. Right in between verses 15 and 17, Paul wrote, "For the Lord himself shall descend from heaven with a shout, with the voice of the archangel, and with the trump [or trumpet] of God: and the dead in Christ shall rise first" (1 Thessalonians 4:16). *Left Behind* describes this event as silent and secret, yet doesn't it seem rather loud and visible? There is a shout, a voice, and a trumpet. Have you ever heard of a silent trumpet? Some people have even called 1 Thessalonians 4:16 the noisiest verse in the Bible!

Now let's put verses 16 and 17 together: "The Lord himself shall descend from heaven with a shout, with the voice of the archangel, and with the trump of God: and the dead in Christ shall rise first. Then we which are alive and remain shall be caught up together with them in the clouds, to meet the Lord in the air: and so shall we ever be with the Lord." Honestly, do you see anything in these words about *vanishing Christians* prior to the Tribulation? Does "caught up" necessarily mean "disappear without a trace"? At the end of His earthly life, Jesus Christ was also "taken up," (Acts 1:9), but this doesn't mean He disappeared, leaving His clothes on earth. Instead, in full view of His wondering disciples, *"while they beheld*, he was taken up; and a cloud received Him out of their sight" (Acts 1:9). Just as Christ's ascension was highly visible, even so do Paul's words about a shout, a voice, a trumpet, a resurrection, and believers being "caught up" into the clouds seem quite visible. That is, if we take them literally.

Let's return to 1 Thessalonians and take a look at the entire context: "For the Lord himself shall descend from heaven with a shout, with the voice of the archangel, and with the trump of God: and the dead in Christ shall rise first. Then we which are alive and remain shall be caught up together with them in the clouds, to meet the Lord in the air: and so shall we ever be with the Lord. Wherefore comfort one another with these words. But of the times and the seasons, brethren, ye have no need that I write unto you. For yourselves know perfectly that the day of the Lord so cometh as *a thief in the night.* For when they shall say, Peace and safety; then sudden destruction will come upon them, as travail upon a woman with child, and they shall not escape." (4:16–5:3, emphasis added).

Paul said this tremendous "day of the Lord" will finally arrive like "a thief in the night." The producers of *Left Behind* interpret this to mean that Jesus will come like a *silent* thief to steal believers out of this world before the seven years of Tribulation — then driverless cars will crash, pilotless planes will collide, and babies will be found missing from their cribs. After this the Antichrist will rise, the Mark of the Beast will come, and people will yet have a second chance to be saved. The popular Christian film, *A Thief in the Night,* which is similar to *LEFT BEHIND: The Movie,* also presents this perspective. Yet is this really what Paul is saying?

Again, let's slow down and take a closer look at our Biblical speedometers. Paul wrote, "You yourselves know perfectly that the day of the Lord will come like a thief in the night. For when they shall say, Peace and safety; then sudden destruction comes upon them, as travail upon a woman with child, and they shall not escape" (1 Thessalonians 5:2, 3). *Do you see what Paul is really saying?* Jesus' coming as a "thief in the night" does not mean He will come quietly and invisibly to steal believers out of this world, as is taught in *Left Behind.* Rather, it means He will come unexpectedly, bringing "sudden destruction" upon the unsaved. *Thus it is not a secret coming, but only a sudden one.* And what about the unprepared being given a second chance to be saved? Paul clearly answered this question when he wrote, *"They shall not escape"* (verse 3).

Therefore, upon the closest examination, the

most widely quoted passage in the Bible used to support the *Left Behind* idea of a silent return of Jesus Christ, of vanishing Christians, and of people being given a second chance during a subsequent period of Tribulation, *doesn't really say this at all!* Paul said Jesus will literally *come down from heaven* with a noisy shout, a loud voice, and with the blast of a trumpet. This awesome and tremendous "day of the Lord" will come unexpectedly upon all the lost like a thief in the night, resulting in their *"sudden* destruction." The apostle Peter also wrote about this same return of Jesus Christ as a thief: "But the day of the Lord will come as *a thief in the night, in the which* the heavens shall pass away with *a great noise,* and the elements shall melt with fervent heat, the earth also and the works that are therein shall be burned up" (2 Peter 3:10, emphasis added). According to Peter, the return of Jesus as a thief is definitely not a silent and secret event before any seven-year period of Tribulation. Rather, this day arrives suddenly, with "a great noise," and is clearly associated with the end of the world! A major crack is starting to form in Pillar 1.

Now let's go back to that mysterious Greek word, "parousia." There is absolutely no doubt that Paul used this word to describe the coming of Jesus at which believers will be "caught up" (1 Thessalonians 4:15–17). This same Greek word is also used in a sizzling apocalyptic message given by Jesus Christ Himself in Matthew 24, so we need to take a look at it. On a certain momentous day, "And as he sat upon the Mount of Olives, his disciples came unto him privately, saying, 'Tell us, when shall these things be? and what shall be the sign of *thy coming,* and of *the end of the world?'"* (Matthew 24:3, emphasis added). The Greek word there in verse 3 for "coming" is "parousia." The disciples associated this "coming," or "parousia," with "the end of the world," and they were anxious to know more about it.

The immediate response of Jesus was: "Take heed that no man deceive you" (Matthew 24:4). The forcefulness of this thought should hit us like a hurricane! Why? Because it clearly implies that when it comes to this exact topic of the "coming" or "parousia" of Jesus Christ and the end of the world, there is going to be a great deal of deception whirling around. And what is even more dramatic is that Jesus raised His "Don't Be Deceived" warning flag *four times* in this single sermon (Matthew 24: 4, 5, 11, 24). One gets the idea that last-day delusions would someday sweep over planet Earth like a massive tidal wave. The only way to avoid being swept away in this swirling sea of falsehood is to pay close attention to the words of Jesus Christ.

Our Lord continued, "For there shall arise false Christs and false prophets, and shall shew great signs and wonders; insomuch that, if it were possible, they shall deceive the very elect" (Matthew 24:24). Here Jesus said Satan's delusions will eventually become so subtle and powerful that only "the elect" will come through unscathed. But who are "the elect"? Based on the context, they must be a group of people who know Jesus Christ and the Bible so well that the devil can't mislead them. Verse 31 also tells us that "the elect" are people who are ready for the return of Jesus Christ.

Immediately after warning about tricky false prophets and deception, Jesus Christ said, "Wherefore if they say unto you, Behold, he is in the desert; go not forth: behold, he is in the *secret* chambers; believe it not. For as the lightning cometh out of the east, and shineth even unto the west; so shall also the coming of the Son of man be" (Matthew 24:26, 27, emphasis added). Here Jesus draws a razor-sharp contrast between false views of His return and the truth. When it comes to false views, don't miss that little word "secret." Jesus plainly warned that people will mistakenly "say" His coming will be in "secret." In fact, based on the context, we discover that this will be one of those powerful delusions which only God's faithful elect will avoid. So how should we respond when people say Jesus' coming will be in secret? Christ's answer is stunning. Jesus said, *"Believe it not"*! Why? Because "as the lightning cometh out of the east, and shineth even unto the west; so shall also the coming of the Son of man be."

Far from being a secret event, the return of Jesus Christ will be like the brilliant flashing of millions of lightning bolts blazing across the sky. Can you guess what awesome Greek word Matthew used for "coming" in verse 27? It is *"parousia,"* and this mega-important word is the exact same word Paul used in 1 Thessalonians 4:15–17 in his description of that coming of Jesus at which believers will be raptured or "caught up"! In many Hollywood action films, certain files are labeled "Top Secret," yet when it comes to Bible truth about the "coming," or "parousia" of Jesus Christ, this return will be *anything but secret.* The crack in Pillar 1 is getting bigger.

Paul plainly said that the Rapture would take place at the "coming" or "parousia" of Jesus Christ (1 Thessalonians 4:15–17). Jesus Himself said His "coming" or "parousia" will be like the brilliant flashing of electrically-charged bolts of lightning hurtling across the sky. The disciples associated this very same awesome "coming" or "parousia" with "the end of the world," and they asked Jesus what the major "sign" of this "coming" would be (Matthew 24:3). After warning about "secret" coming ideas and deception, Jesus finally answered this exact question by lifting the curtain of history and fully unveiling what His high-powered and super-cataclysmic "coming" or "parousia" will really be like: "And then shall appear the sign of the Son of man in heaven: and then shall all the tribes of the earth mourn, and they shall see the Son of man coming in the clouds of heaven with power and great glory. And he shall send his angels with a great sound of a trumpet, and they shall gather together his elect from the four winds, from one end of heaven to the other" (Matthew 24:30, 31).

This high-impact description of Christ's return contains an even Bigger Bang than the highly-speculative evolutionary Big Bang theory. The "coming" or "parousia" of Jesus Christ, *at which believers will* be *"caught up,"* will be unmistakably *visible* to "all the tribes of the earth." The amazed masses of mankind will literally *"see* the Son of man coming in the clouds of heaven with power and great glory." Certainly no one will miss it, and no one will wake up the next day wondering where all the Christians went. On that great day, all the unsaved will "mourn." Why? Not because their loved ones have vanished into thin air, but because Jesus Christ has *suddenly come,* and now their life of sinning and partying is over. And once again, this will be a very noisy and loud event that will include the echoing of "a great sound of a trumpet" throughout the sky. When that booming blast is heard, billions of shining angels will descend and circle the globe to *"gather together* his elect from the four winds." Thus, true believers will be "caught up" into the air. Now don't miss it. These are the very same elements Paul wrote about in 1 Thessalonians 4:17!

In *both* Matthew 24:30, 31, and in 1 Thessalonians 4:16, 17, we read about clouds, noise, a trumpet, a gathering together, and believers being transported up into the air. Any concordance will show you that *both* passages refer to the "coming" or "parousia" of Jesus Christ. In Matthew 24:27, 30, 31, this "coming" or "parousia" *unmistakably* applies to Christ's "Glorious Appearing." As we are to be "caught up together," let's put these shocking pieces together. The conclusion is inescapable, unalterable, and irrefutable. True believers will be "caught up" or "raptured" at the loud, climactic, highly-visible, and ultra-glorious Second Coming of Jesus Christ!

This book is like a race car whose engine is just beginning to rev up. We have a lot more to cover, so let's keep going. In Matthew 24, after describing His "Glorious Appearing," Jesus continued: "But of *that day* and hour knoweth no man, no, not the angels of heaven, but my Father only. But as the days of Noe were, so shall also the coming of the Son of man be. For as in the days that were before the flood they were eating and drinking, marrying and giving in marriage, until the day that Noe entered the ark, And knew not until the flood came, and took them all away; so shall also the coming of the Son of man be. *Then* shall two be in the field; the one shall be taken and the other left. Two women shall be grinding at the mill; the one shall be taken and the other left. Watch therefore: for ye know not what hour your Lord doth come. But know this, that if the goodman of the house had known in what watch the thief would come, he would have watched, and would not have suffered his house to be broken up. Therefore be ye also ready: for in such an hour as you think not, the Son of man cometh" (Matthew 24:36–44, emphasis added).

Here Jesus Christ paralleled His return with the sudden descent of billions of tons of water upon the lost in Noah's day. Those ancient people thought Noah was a crazy old man, until "the flood came, and took them all away; so shall also *the coming* of the Son of man be" (Matthew 24:39, emphasis added). Can you guess what Greek word is used here again for "coming?" Don't take my word for it, but look it up yourself in your own concordance. It is *"parousia,"* which, as we have already proven, clearly applies to the visible "Glorious Appearing" of Jesus Christ. Now notice, *immediately* after the word "parousia" is used in verse 39, Jesus continued: "THEN shall two be in the field; the one shall be taken and the other left (emphasis added)." This is probably the second most quoted passage in the Bible now being used to support the *Left Behind* idea of a silent Rapture prior to the Tribulation. Supposedly, when this verse is fulfilled, those who are "taken" will vanish without a trace, leaving only their clothes, shoes, false teeth and wedding rings, while those who are "left" will have to endure the Tribulation, facing the Antichrist and the Mark. But is this really what Jesus Christ is saying?

The correct answer to this question will not come by depending on the interpretations of others. Actually, it is never safe to lean wholly on any man. Christians should never be taught to rely completely on Tim LaHaye, Jerry Jenkins, or any other popular teacher, including Steve Wohlberg. We should all open our own Bibles, pick up our own concordances, and find out for ourselves what is truth. If you are willing to do this, then this is what you will most definitely find — believers will be "taken" (verse 40) at the "coming" or "parousia" (verse 39) which the Bible clearly applies to the loud, highly-visible, and ultra-glorious Second Coming of Jesus Christ at the end of the world (Matthew 24:3, 27, 30, 31, 39)!

Jesus basically said, "It will be just like Noah's day" (verses 37–39). Now think about it. Did Noah and his family vanish before the flood? No, they walked visibly into the ark. And what about those who were *left behind* after the door of the ark was shut? Did they have a second chance? No again. How were they left? *They were left dead; they did not escape.* After saying, "the flood came, and took them all away," Jesus made His power-packed point, "so shall also the coming ["parousia"] of the Son of man be" (verse 39). And then, without a break, Christ said, "*Then* shall two be in the field; the one shall be taken and the other left" (verse 40). Upon careful analysis, these words leave no room for the continuing lives of *Left Behind's* Rayford Steele and Buck Williams during the Tribulation after the Rapture. Why not? Because those who are "taken" are taken up at the "coming" or "parousia," which applies to the final Second Coming of Jesus Christ!

Immediately after saying, "One shall be taken and the other left," the King of the Universe then compared His Second Coming to the sudden arrival of a midnight thief, just like Paul did in 1 Thessalonians 5:2, 3. Jesus said: "But know this, if the goodman of the house had known in what watch the thief would come, he would have watched, and would not have suffered his house to be broken up. Therefore be ye also ready: for in such an hour as you think not, the Son of man cometh" (Matthew 24:43, 44). To "watch" doesn't mean spending endless hours in front of the television set, nor does it mean watching popular movies about the end times that may take detours away from the straight truth. Rather, it means to *watch out for deception!*

Matthew 24 and 1 Thessalonians 4 and 5 fit together just as perfectly as Adam and Eve before they sinned. Both describe a noisy, loud, highly visible, trumpet-blasting and ultra-glorious return of Jesus Christ in the clouds. Both describe believers being caught up and transported into the air. Both declare this day will come with thief-like suddenness upon all sleeping sinners. In Noah's day, when billions of tons of water came crashing down, there were no second chances for those outside the ark. Paul said the lost "shall not escape." And both Paul and Matthew use the exact same Greek word to describe this great, tremendous, and awesomely powerful "day of the Lord." Simply look in your concordance. That word is "parousia," which clearly refers to the Second Coming of Jesus Christ. True believers are urged to watch, be ready, and to avoid all subtle, satanic deceptions.

What about the Rapture taking place "in a moment, in the twinkling of an eye"? This is probably the third most quoted passage in the Bible now being used to support the idea of vanishing Christians prior to the Tribulation. We have previously slowed down to look at our Biblical speedometers, yet this time we must come to a screeching halt. Paul wrote, "Behold, I shew you a mystery; We shall not all sleep, but we shall all be changed. In a moment, in the twinkling of an eye, *at the last trump: for the trumpet shall sound,* and the dead shall be raised incorruptible, and we shall be changed" (1 Corinthians 15:51, 52, emphasis added). Is Paul saying that believers will mysteriously vanish from the earth prior to the Tribulation, while their loved ones blink? Not at all! He is saying that the dead will be raised and our bodies will be changed "in a moment, in the twinkling of an eye." But *when* will this "moment" take place? Paul's answer is clear. It will occur *"at the last trump,"* when "the trumpet shall sound," that is, at the end of the world. This is that very same "great sound of a trumpet" Jesus said would be heard at His Second Coming (Matthew 24:31)! Pillar 1 is cracking and crumbling.

As we have previously noted, Pillar 2 supporting the *Left Behind* house is the theory that those who miss the Rapture will have a *second chance* to be saved during the Tribulation. If you think about it, this idea can be dangerous. Some might rationalize, "If the Rapture really takes place, then I'll know for sure God is real. It may be tough, but I can still join the Tribulation Force during the seven years. Even if that Antichrist guy tries to kill me, I will still resist the Mark!" While the fostering of this foolish attitude is not the intent of *Left Behind*, people can easily adopt this "let's wait and see" position, *putting off their decision to follow Jesus Christ.* But Paul wrote that all who are not fully on the Lord's side when believers are "caught up…shall not escape" (1 Thessalonians 4:17; 5:3), and there were no second chances in Noah's day. After the door of the ark closed, all desperate attempts to get inside were useless. Therefore Pillar 2 is becoming like a man diagnosed with cancer — it has very serious problems.

If Pillars 1 and 2 supporting the *Left Behind*

house are wrong, and if the logical alternative about the Church being "caught up" at the Second Coming of Jesus Christ is right, then this means that the Church of today is destined to go through the Tribulation, rather than disappearing before it arrives. Yet Christians often resist this conclusion with the argument, "God wouldn't allow us to go through the Tribulation because He loves us too much!" But think about it. Does He love us any more than He would love the Tribulation Force after the Rapture? Obviously not. Then why would He allow them to go through such a period? Could it be that the doctrine of *escaping tribulation* is really only catering to our middle-class American tendencies? We like comfort and hate to go through trials, and we can hardly bear it when our TV-dinner lifestyle is threatened. Yet historically, God's people have gone through intense suffering. All of the disciples of Jesus, except for John, were cruelly murdered. Thousands of the early Christians were literally torn to shreds by wild dogs and lions inside the Coliseum. Millions of others were horribly tortured by the Inquisition and burned to ashes during the Dark Ages. Believers in Russia and China have suffered terribly under Communism, and yet American Christians say, "God wouldn't allow us go through the Tribulation"!

When it comes to this topic of "tribulation," once again, concordances can come in handy. If you look up the word, "tribulation," in a *Strong's* or *Young's Concordance*, you may be shocked to discover that almost every reference describes *the suf-*

fering of believers. Jesus told His followers, "In the world ye shall have *tribulation"* (John 16:33). Paul told his early Christian converts, "...we must through much *tribulation* enter the kingdom of God" (Acts 14:22). Paul wrote to the Church at Thessalonica, "...we ourselves boast of you among the churches of God for your patience and faith in all your persecutions and *tribulations* that you endure" (2 Thessalonians 1:4). On the lonely isle of Patmos, John was our "brother and companion in *tribulation"* (Revelation 1:9). Jesus told His Church in Smyrna, "I know thy works, and *tribulation"* (Revelation 2:9). In the light of these Scriptures, the idea of Christians *escaping tribulation* seems like fantasy and illusion.

Some Christians might respond by saying, "Yes, but those verses are talking about 'tribulation,' not *'the* Tribulation.' " But think about it. If the majority of the Bible's "tribulation texts" refer to what believers *go through,* why would God's Word suddenly shift gears by teaching that *"the* Tribulation" is something believers will *not* go through? Even in *Left Behind,* there are Christians who do go through *"the* Tribulation" (the Tribulation Force), therefore the thought of Christians going through this period is really not so strange.

Many Christians also argue, "If the Church is going through the Tribulation, then why isn't the Church mentioned after Revelation 4?" Let's take a closer look. In Revelation 4:1, John was told to "come up hither." People conclude this represents the Rapture and they think the Church isn't mentioned anymore. First of all, John did not actually go to heaven in Revelation 4:1, he was simply taken up *in a vision,* while his toes were still on Patmos. Secondly, the Church *is* on earth after Revelation 4. How do we know this? Because the Bible says the Antichrist will make "war with *the saints*" (13:7), then we read about "*the faith of the saints*" (13:10), and then, during the Mark of the Beast crisis, Revelation refers to "*the saints*" who keep "*the faith of Jesus*" (14:12). Some might respond by saying, "Yes, but those are the Tribulation saints after the Rapture, not the Church." But consider this. Paul wrote his New Testament letters to the "churches of the saints" (1 Corinthians 14:33). What does this tell us? It tells us that wherever there are saints, *there is the Church!* Even if the saints mentioned in Revelation 13 and 14 are only the Tribulation saints after the Rapture, wouldn't they, as sincere believers in Jesus Christ, *still be the Church?*

Left Behind teaches that the Church will not be here for Armageddon. Is this true? The word "Armageddon" occurs in Revelation 16:16, which is the great chapter about the falling of the seven last plagues. Right before verse 16, *during* the time of the seven last plagues, Jesus Christ thunders, "Behold, I come as a thief. Blessed is he that watches and keeps his garments, lest he walk naked and they see his shame. And he gathered them together into a place called in the Hebrew tongue, Armageddon" (Revelation 16:15, 16). Did you catch that? Who is Jesus talking to? To the Church! At the time of verse 15, *while* the seven plagues are falling, which is definitely *during* the Tribulation, and right before the battle of Armageddon, Jesus Christ has not yet come as a thief! Therefore He must come like a thief *at Armageddon, after* the Tribulation, and this must be the time when He comes to gather His Church.

Like a good Commanding Officer, Paul urged the soldiers of the cross, "Wherefore take unto you the whole armour of God, that you may be able to withstand in the evil day, and having done all, to stand" (Ephesians 6:13). How can we stand in "the evil day" if we have previously disappeared? Jesus Christ also said, "But he that shall endure to the end, the same shall be saved" (Matthew 24:13). So how long must we endure? *To the end.* Yet Christ will be with us, that's why He promised, "I am with you alway, even unto the end of the world" (Matthew 28:20). We can trust Him in this.

If everything in this book is true, then what about "the seven years"? The concept of a seven-year period of Tribulation is actually the underlying foundation of the entire *Left Behind* scenario. Remember, the theory is that first the Rapture takes place, and then comes the seven years of Tribulation. Book Two of the *Left Behind* novels declares, "The disappearances have ushered in the seven-year period of Tribulation" (*The Tribulation Force*, inside cover). Book Three reveals, "...the seven-year Tribulation is nearing the end of its first quarter..." (Nicolae, inside cover). Book Six tells us, "It's the midpoint of the seven-year Tribulation" (*The Indwelling,* inside cover). Book Eight begins with "...the dawn of the second half of the seven-year Tribulation..." (*The Mark*, inside cover). Thus this New York Times and Wall Street Journal best-selling series of Christian books, now being endorsed by well-respected Church leaders nationwide, is built completely around this seven-year framework.

The Great Granddaddy Bible Text for the entire seven-year Tribulation theory is Daniel 9:27. This passage is the very first verse quoted in *LEFT BEHIND: The Movie.* Here is what it says: "And he shall confirm the covenant with many for *one week,* and in the midst of the week he shall cause the sacrifice...to cease." A day in prophecy represents a year (Numbers 14:34, Ezekiel 4:6), thus this famous period of "one week" actually represents seven years. Millions are now applying this to a future seven-year period of Tribulation. "He" is interpreted to be the Antichrist who will make a covenant with the Jews during the Tribulation. Book 6 of the *Left Behind* novels is called *Assassins.* The subtitle reads, "Assignment: Jerusalem, Target: Antichrist." Its focus is "the half-way point of the Global Community's seven-year protection agreement with Israel" (p. 302).

According to *Left Behind,* immediately after the Rapture, the Antichrist will make this "seven-year protection agreement with Israel." Yet I wonder how he could accomplish this so quickly right after the Rapture, for wouldn't he need some time to rise to power? An intrinsic part of this story is the theory that, during the Tribulation, the Jewish temple will be rebuilt and animal sacrifices will be resumed (more on this later). Supposedly, half-way into the

Tribulation, the Antichrist will break his "protection agreement" with the Jews and stop the sacrifices, thereby causing them "to cease." This is how millions of Christians today are now interpreting Daniel 9:27.

What many don't realize is that there is another reasonable interpretation that is quite different. Not only does this alternate view have a great deal of Biblical support, but it has also been taught in the past by many credible Bible scholars who have written respected commentaries which are now in the libraries of pastors across America. One example is the world-famous *Matthew Henry's Bible Commentary.* Shockingly, this commentary doesn't apply Daniel 9:27 to the Antichrist at all, nor does it apply the "one week" to a seven-year period of Tribulation after the Rapture. Rather, it applies it *to Jesus Christ,* who, after three and one-half years of loving ministry, died "in the midst of the week," which ultimately caused all animal sacrifices to cease!

Here's the quotation from Matthew Henry's famous commentary: "By offering himself a sacrifice once and for all he [Jesus] shall put an end to all Levitical sacrifices" (*Matthew Henry's Commentary on the Whole Bible,* Vol. IV — Isaiah to Malachi, Complete Edition. New York: Fleming H. Revell Co., 1712, Notes on Daniel 9:27, p. 1095). Another excellent Bible commentary written by the well known British Methodist, Adam Clarke, says, "This confirmation of the covenant must take in the ministry of John the Baptist with that of our Lord, comprehending the term of seven years, during the whole of which he might well be said to confirm or ratify the new covenant with mankind" (*The Holy Bible with a commentary and critical notes* by Adam Clarke, Vol. IV — Isaiah to Malachi. New York: Abingdon-Cokesbury Press, Notes on Daniel 9:27, p. 602). Here's one more from the much-respected *Jamieson, Fausset and Brown Commentary*: "He shall confirm the covenant — Christ. The confirmation of the covenant is assigned to Him" (Rev. Robert Jamieson, Rev. A. R. Fausset. and Rev. David Brown, *A Commentary Critical and Explanatory on the Whole Bible,* Complete Edition. Hartford, CT: S.S. Scranton Co., Notes on Daniel 9:27, p. 641). All of these commentaries are now available electronically on the World Wide Web, so you can easily check these references yourself.

Which view is right — the one put forth in *Left Behind,* or the one described in those old dusty commentaries? Does Daniel 9:27 apply to a future seven year period of Tribulation, or was it fulfilled by Jesus Christ 2000 years ago? The only way to find out is by taking a careful look at Daniel 9:27 itself. God's Word says, "And he shall confirm the *covenant* with *many.*" Now take a look at this. Jesus Christ Himself said, "For this is my blood of the new *covenant,* which is shed for *many*" (Matthew 26:28, New King James version). Behold a perfect fit! Both use the words "covenant" and "many." Popular teaching says the Antichrist will make a covenant or "protection agreement" with the Jews and then break it after three and one-half years, yet the Bible actually says, "He shall *confirm* the covenant with many *for one week."* Thus "He" is to *confirm* the covenant for the full seven years, not break it! And it is not simply "a covenant," as is commonly understood. No! It is *"the covenant"* which applies to the New Covenant. Our Lord Jesus Christ is the one by whom *"the covenant,...was confirmed"* (Galatians 3:17; see also Romans 15:8). In "the midst of the week," after three and one-half years, Jesus gave His life for us, "causing the sacrifice to cease." He was the final sacrifice. No more sacrifices are to be offered. Period. (Hebrews 10:12).

In my other book, *Exploding the Israel Deception,* Chapter 5 is called "The 70th Week of Daniel Delusion" (see the back of this book for details). There I give many more solid reasons why Daniel 9:27 doesn't apply to the Antichrist at all, but to Jesus Christ alone. The fact is, the entire *Left Behind* idea of a seven-year period of Tribulation after the Rapture is a grand illusion, a massive megamyth. It may even go down in history as the Greatest Evangelical Misinterpretation of All Time! The whole concept is like a gigantic bubble. Once Daniel 9:27 is correctly understood, and the sharply-pointed pin of truth is inserted, "Pop! goes the seven years!"

I want to conclude this chapter by talking about Pillar 3 which now supports the *Left Behind* house — The Church of today will *escape the Tribulation* and will *not* have to face the Antichrist and the Mark of the Beast. This is the Big One, and it is right here that emotions fly and reason vanishes just as quickly as those disappearing people in *LEFT BEHIND: The*

Movie. Why? The answer is simple. If Pillar 3 is false, and if the Church will not be "caught up" until the Second Coming of Jesus Christ, then this obviously means that the Church must *first* pass through Earth's final period of Tribulation, and will have to face the Antichrist and the Mark. Many Christians fear such a conclusion, and this is why, many times, underneath the attempt to maintain the doctrine of a Pre-Tribulation *Secret* Rapture, there often lurks a *secret* fear of having to face the Mark of the Beast.

This reminds me of the tragic deaths of 118 crewmen inside the giant Russian nuclear submarine, Kursk. On Saturday, August 12, 2000, way out in the icy waters of the Barents Sea, east-northeast of Moscow, something went terribly wrong. An explosion took place, which was followed by another. The "catastrophe developed at lightning speed," (*Newsweek,* Nov. 6, 2000. p. 43) and the doomed sub quickly sank to the bottom of the ocean. *Newsweek* ran a story on this called, "A Cry From the Deep." Twenty-three Russians survived the initial blasts and flooding. A letter was later found by deep-sea divers inside a pocket of one of the corpses. The note said, "There are 23 people here….None of us can get to the surface" (*Newsweek,* Nov. 6, 2000. p. 43). Because help didn't come quickly enough, they all died. As I have thought about this, I can imagine the *feeling of fear* in the hearts of those Russian sailors deep down below the calm surface of the water.

Fear also lurks below the doctrine of a Pre-

Tribulation Rapture. Deep down underneath the surface of many arguments, lies a hidden fear of having to face the Mark of the Beast. This fear may be unconscious, yet often it is there, though it need not be. True Christians can learn a lesson from popular bumper stickers which say, "Fear No Evil." We don't need to be afraid. We can trust in Jesus Christ, for hasn't He promised, "Lo, I am with you alway, even unto the end of the world"? (Matthew 28:20). If the fictitious Tribulation Force in the *Left Behind* novels can overcome the Antichrist and the Mark of the Beast, *then so can we!* Yet Christians *do* fear the Mark, and this fear often prevents them from even reasonably examining the clear Scriptural evidence in favor of a Post-Tribulation gathering of the Church to Christ. And thus, sadly, the Pre-Tribulation Rapture idea has become The Great Evangelical Escape Clause for the Avoidance of the Mark of the Beast! And for those who must have it that way, no amount of Biblical evidence will convince them. Like a triple-bolted door in downtown New York, they are simply closed to the facts.

The result? *Truth is left behind.*

Chapter 2
Unmasking the Antichrist

When most Christians think about the Antichrist, they usually think about one super-sinister individual who will rise to power in Europe after the Rapture. The fictitious Nicolae Carpathia, the Antichrist in the *Left Behind* novels, is a perfect example of such thinking. Nicolae Carpathia is portrayed as a brilliant Romanian, an astute politician, a born leader, "one of the most powerful and charismatic personalities ever" (*The Tribulation Force*, p. ix). He quickly seizes power after the Rapture, takes control of the United Nations, and establishes a one-world government during the Tribulation. He speaks gentle and compassionate words to the masses, yet he is secretly "indwelt by the devil himself." Underneath his warm and winning exterior, lies hidden "the monster within." After he becomes the "Supreme Potentate, His Excellency Nicolae Carpathia," the world openly worships him as God (*The Mark — The Beast Rules the World*, inside cover; p. 2; xi).

Because most Christians firmly believe the Antichrist will be a single person like Carpathia, and because millions sense the Rapture is near, some are even now speculating as to who this inwardly devilish Antichrist might be. In the last few years, some have suggested Prince Charles of England, others Mikhail Gorbechev, and still others Bill Gates, the founder of Microsoft. One person even went so far as to suggest that the Antichrist might be David Hasselhoff, the star of the incredibly popular television series *Baywatch*, filmed at the Pacific Ocean. In *Baywatch*, David plays a lifeguard named Mitch. Because Revelation 13:1 describes the Beast as coming out of the sea, David seems to this person like a perfect fit! Of course hardly anyone has taken this seriously. But the fact remains: Christians everywhere are definitely expecting someone sinister to rise up as the Antichrist. One man. A mysterious, evil person.

What does the Bible really say about the Antichrist? The word "antichrist" or "antichrists" is only used five times in the New Testament, and these are all found in 1 and 2 John. We are about to begin an awesome journey into one of the most misunderstood of all Bible subjects. It is super-hot, yet here we go. Almost 2,000 years ago, John wrote: "Little children, it is the last time: and as you have heard that antichrist shall come, even now are there many antichrists; whereby we know that it is the last time. They went out from us" (1 John 2:18,19).

Do you realize what you just read? John's points are more explosive than an erupting volcano. Here's a simple summary:

(1) The early Christians had heard that antichrist was coming.
(2) Even now many antichrists have come.
(3) This is evidence that "the last time" is here.
(4) These antichrists "went out from us."

This is truth stranger than fiction. When most Christians think about the Antichrist, they think of only one sinister person like Carpathia, yet John said there are "many antichrists." When most Christians think about the Antichrist coming, they place this development only in the future after the Rapture. But John wrote that many antichrists are here "even now." When most Christians think about the Antichrist, they think he will only appear during that "seven-year period called the Tribulation" (*The Tribulation Force,* inside cover). Yet John said "the last time" *is here now!*

When most people think about the Antichrist, they think of a blatantly anti-Christian individual who will openly make war against a group of post-Rapture people like the Tribulation Force. But John said, "They went out from *us"*(1 John 2:19, emphasis added). What does this mean? John uses the word "us" in reference to himself and other Christians of the early Church. In other words, the antichrists John was describing were rising up from *inside of Chris-*

tianity! According to John, many antichrists are already here, the last time has come, and these antichrists have come out from *within* the Christian Church. Does Nicolae Carpathia pass these Biblical tests? Like an "F" on a final exam, he fails *at every point.*

Again John wrote, "Who is a liar, but he that denieth that Jesus is the Christ? He is antichrist, that denieth the Father and the Son....These things I have written to you concerning them that *seduce* you." (1 John 2:22, 26, emphasis added). These words are of mega-importance. The Antichrist will deny the Father and the Son, yet this denial will be *seductive,* not obvious. Let's examine this. Jesus said, "I am the way, the truth, and the life. No one comes to the Father, but by Me" (John 14:6). The Father is God. Jesus, the Son, is the only way to the Father. Paul also wrote, "There is one God and one mediator between God and men, the Man Christ Jesus" (1 Timothy 2:5). Our Heavenly Father loves us, that's why He sent Jesus, His only Son. As trusting children, we can come to our Heavenly Father directly through Jesus Christ. We don't need any other mediator or go-between, for His loving arms are open wide. And this mediator is "the Man Christ Jesus," *not a woman.*

Again John warned, "Every spirit that confesseth not that Jesus Christ is come in the flesh is not of God: and this is that spirit of antichrist, whereof you have heard that it should come, and even now already is it in the world. Ye are of God, little children, and have overcome them: because greater is he that is in you, than he that is in the world" (1 John 4:3, 4). Thus the Antichrist will deny that Jesus Christ has come in *"the flesh."* What does His coming in the flesh mean? First, it means that Jesus is fully human. He loves us and understands us completely. Next, because Jesus has come in "*the* flesh," He is now "*the* way, *the* truth, and *the* life" (John 14:6). No one comes to the Father, but through Him. He is our only Mediator, *"the* Man Christ Jesus"* (1 Timothy 2:5). This is why we don't need any other mediators. Yet the Antichrist will deny this, though not obviously, but seductively.

And again, did John look for this Antichrist only in the future during the Tribulation? No, for he wrote, "…ye have heard that it should come, and even now already is *it* in the world" (1 John 4:3). According to John, "it" is here now, and "it" *is more than one single person like Nicolae Carpathia.* There is a mysterious "spirit of antichrist." And who is to fight this? John wrote, "*Ye* [you] are of God, little children, and have overcome them" (verse 4). Question: Who is to "overcome" these many antichrists? Answer: True Christians! The Bible says, *"You!"* Yet this is entirely contrary to *Left Behind's* idea that Christians today will not have to face the Antichrist because he comes only after the Rapture. Is something "seductive" going on around here?

What I am about to say may shock you, yet it's entirely true. The current wildly popular idea of a one-man Antichrist like Nicolae Carpathia who comes only after the Rapture is a *new doctrine,* at least when it comes to Protestants. From the 1500s, down to the early 1900s, the majority of Baptists, Methodists, Congregationalists, Lutherans, Anglicans, Presbyterians, and Mennonites believed, based on a careful study of Scripture, that the Bible's predictions about "antichrist" (1 John 2 and 4); "the little horn" (Daniel 7); "that man of sin" (2 Thessalonians 2); "the Mother of Harlots" (Revelation 17); and "the beast" (Revelation 13) *all apply most specifically to the Roman Catholic Church. Newsweek* has reported, "Martin Luther was the first to identify the papacy as such with the Antichrist. At first he discounted the value of John's Apocalypse. But then he saw in it a revelation of the Church of Rome as the deceiving Antichrist…a view that was to become dogma for all Protestant churches" (*Newsweek,* Nov. 1, 1999, p. 72).

"Wycliffe, Tyndale, Luther, Calvin, Cranmer; in the seventeenth century, Bunyan, the translators of the King James Bible and the men who published the Westminster and Baptist Confessions of Faith; Sir Isaac Newton, John Wesley, Whitfield, Jonathan Edwards; and more recently, Spurgeon, Bishop J.C. Ryle and Dr. Martyn Lloyd-Jones; these men among countless others, all saw the office of the Papacy as the antichrist.…The Reformers and their heirs were great scholars and knew the Word of God and the Holy Spirit as a living teacher (*All Roads Lead to Rome,* Michael de Semlyen. Dorchester House Publications, 1991. pp. 205, 206). If any of these ancient Christian scholars could somehow have been transported into a 21st century theater showing *LEFT BEHIND: The Movie,* they would have wondered, "What's this all about?"

In this little book, I am going to talk plainly about Protestants and Catholics, but first I want to make a few things clear. I have no desire to attack individuals on either side. I fully believe many Catholics will be in the kingdom, and I hope to join them. Catholics are now helping tens of thousands of people through orphanages and in many other ways. People are people, and every one of us is deeply loved by Jesus Christ, no matter what church we belong to. I also recognize contemporary Catholicism's diversity, and that millions of American Catholics do not subscribe to all of the doctrines of the Vatican. Many are searching. Yet I am also a student of prophecy who shares the view of the major Protestant Reformers. I do not apply the words of Daniel, Paul, and Revelation to individual Catholics, but rather to *the papal system as a whole* with its still current doctrines about many heavenly mediators (Mary and the saints), forgiveness only through priests, purgatory, and no salvation outside of the Mother Church.

Jesus Christ is the only way to the Father (John 14:6). There is only one Mediator up there in heaven, and it is "the Man Christ Jesus" (1 Timothy 2:5). "Believe on the Lord Jesus Christ, and thou shalt be saved" (Acts 16:31). These are solid Bible facts. Yet historically, and at present, these truths are still officially denied by the Vatican. Catholics are still sincerely and yet mistakenly being taught to look to Mary and to many other saints as mediators. To date, the Roman Catholic Church still does not accept the idea that Christians can be saved by faith in Jesus

Christ without going through the Church. *Who really is the Beast of prophecy?* Will it be someone like Nicolae Carpathia, or was Martin Luther correct? Why did the belief that Papal Rome was the Antichrist, "the beast" and "the little horn" become "dogma for all Protestant churches" (*Newsweek,* Nov. 1, 1999, p. 72)? It's time to find out by carefully studying the Bible.

Daniel 2 speaks of four successive kingdoms: Babylon, Persia, Greece, and Rome. There is no question about this anywhere. Daniel 7 also describes four kingdoms, using the symbols of a lion, a bear, a leopard, and a dragon-like beast with ten horns. Daniel 7:23 is a super-important text, so don't miss it. A holy angel told Daniel, "The fourth beast shall be the fourth kingdom upon earth." So, what is a beast in prophecy? Does it represent a single, solitary, devil-indwelt man like Nicolae Carpathia? or possibly some gigantic 5000-gigabyte super-computer? No. According to Daniel 7:23, *a beast represents a kingdom.* Never forget this! This truth is like a gigantic fork in the road. If we make a mistake here, we might end up thinking Bill Gates is the Beast. Daniel 7:23 is truly a foundational text which will save us from global delusions. Based on history and the clear parallels between Daniel 2 and 7, the fourth beast was the Roman Empire.

It's time to focus on "the little horn" of Daniel 7. Catholics, Protestants, and Evangelicals, including the authors of *Left Behind,* all agree this horn represents the Antichrist. It is their *interpretations* of Bible prophecy that vary. Here are nine fast-facts about the little horn in Daniel 7:

(1) The little horn comes out of the fourth beast, that is, out of the Roman Empire (7:7, 8).
(2) It rises "among" the ten horns that divided up that very Empire (7:8).
(3) It comes "after" the ten horns are in place (7:24).
(4) It will be "diverse" or different from the other ten horns (7:24).
(5) It will pluck up "by the roots" three of the first ten horns (7:8).
(6) It has "eyes like the eyes of a man" (7:8).
(7) It has "a mouth speaking great things" (7:8).
(8) It will wage "war with the saints" (7:21).
(9) It will rule for "a time, times and the dividing of time" (7:25).

As surely as George Washington was America's first president, even so are these nine points sure facts in Daniel 7.

When most prophesy teachers today talk about the "little horn," they apply it to someone like Nicolae Carpathia. Most realize the four beasts in Daniel 7 represent Babylon, Persia, Greece, and Rome. But then they do something absolutely amazing—they virtually slice the ten horns and the little horn from off of the head of the fourth beast, and *slide them all down to the end of time.* But this creates an unnatural 1,500-year GAP (more on this later) between the fourth beast, which is the Roman Empire, and the little horn. The truth is, the entire prophecy is orderly, successive, and chronological.

There are four beasts, *then* ten horns, *then* the little horn, with NO GAPS. It is simply not logical, nor Biblical, to slice a 1,500-year hole in the head of the fourth beast!

In Daniel's prophecies "horns" also represent kingdoms (Daniel 8:8, 22). What happened in history? In 476 A.D., the Roman Empire collapsed after being invaded by ten Germanic kingdoms from the north. These kingdoms laid the foundations of the modern nations of Europe — the Alemani (Germany), the Burgundians (Switzerland), the Saxons (England), the Visigoths (Spain), the Franks (France), the Lombards (Italy), and the Suevi (Portugal). The Vandals, the Heruli, and the Ostrogoths also settled in their places. When the Roman imperial government collapsed in 476 A.D., Europe was looking for leadership. Can you guess who rose into supreme political power in the Roman Empire, "among" the ten horns, shortly "after" 476 A.D.? *The Roman Catholic Church.* Papal Rome was "different" because it was not just a political power, but also a religious power. Three of the first ten horns (the Vandals, the Heruli, and the Ostrogoths) resisted Papal Rome's rise to power. As a result of the Vatican's political influence, those three were destroyed and completely *"uprooted"* from history!

Papal Rome has "eyes like the eyes of a man," having human leadership centered in the Pope. It has a "mouth speaking great things" when it claims to be the only true Church, with the very keys of heaven and hell, outside of which there is no salvation. In September 2000, in his 36-page document

Dominus Jesus, Pope John Paul II reaffirmed that there is salvation only in the Roman Church. Quickly the *Los Angeles Times* ran this headline: "Vatican Reiterates Strict Dogma — Roman Catholicism only path to salvation, declaration states." Thus Rome's position has not changed, even in our modern times. It still has "a mouth speaking great things." This Church *did indeed* make "war with the saints" by putting to death approximately 50–100 million so-called "heretics" during the Dark Ages. People today have forgotten about the Crusades, the dark torture chambers of the Inquisition, and the many horrifying massacres of Protestants and Jews. Yet these things really happened. Like a key fitting into a lock, prophecy fits with history. It is also true that history unlocks prophecy.

Outside of Jesus Christ, more books have been written about Martin Luther than any other single religious person in history. How did Martin Luther interpret Daniel 7? Luther wrote that Daniel "saw the terrible wild beast which had ten horns, which by the consent of all is the Roman Empire, he also beheld another *small horn* come up in the middle of them. *This is the Papal power,* which rose up in the middle of the Roman Empire" (*Romanism and the Reformation — From the Standpoint of Prophecy,* H. Grattan Guinness. Harley House, Bow, London. 1891, p. 127. Italics original. See also *Works of Martin Luther,* vol. II, p. 386). As bold and fiery as he was, Martin Luther did not slice a 1,500-year hole in the head of the fourth beast! He saw NO GAP.

Now back to the Beast. A careful study of the

Bible reveals that the Beast of Revelation 13 is the same as the little horn of Daniel 7. Most Catholics, Protestants, and Evangelicals, including the authors of *Left Behind,* agree with this. Again, it is their *interpretations* that vary. Revelation 13 says the Beast will be a composite creature with the characteristics of a lion, a bear, and a leopard (13:2). It also has a mouth (13:5), makes war on the saints (13:7), and rules for forty-two months (13:5), which are all perfect parallels with Daniel 7. But there is something many people have missed, and from a prophetic standpoint, it is a truth more important than avoiding a quadruple bypass surgery. Here it is. Based on the perfect parallels of Revelation 13 with Daniel 7, *a beast represents a kingdom, not one man like Nicolae Carpathia!* And the Roman Catholic Church *is a kingdom,* with over 100 embassies on Vatican Hill.

Revelation 13:2 mentions a lion, a bear, a leopard, and a dragon. While the primary dragon in the Bible is Satan, this verse clearly runs parallel with Daniel 7:3–7. The fourth beast in Daniel 7, which was dragon-like, was the Roman Empire. Revelation 13:2 says the dragon would give *"his seat"* to the Beast. This "seat" does not refer to a physical chair somewhere, but rather to a seat of government. Where was the seat of government of the fourth beast? It was the city of Rome itself, and this is where the Vatican "sits" today! About 1,500 years ago, the Roman Empire gave its seat of government over to the Roman Catholic Church. Notice this quotation from a well-known historian: "Disregarding the maxims and the spirit of the Gospel, the papal Church, arming herself with the power of the sword, vexed the Church of God and wasted it for several centuries, a period most appropriately termed in history, the 'dark ages.' The kings of the earth gave their power to the 'Beast' " (*Fox's Book of Martyrs,* 1926 edition, p. 43).

As this book races down the highway of prophecy, it is essential that we pass through a major intersection — 2 Thessalonians 2. The issues in that chapter are simply too great to pass by. There Paul predicts the rising of *"that man* of sin" (2:3). Doesn't this prove that the Antichrist is one man? That chapter is also used to support the idea of a secret Rapture *prior* to the coming of the Antichrist. Thus, this is a very important, controversial, and high-impact section. As we examine it closely, we will discover some absolutely shocking truths. So put on your seatbelts—here we go.

It is almost unbelievable, but the very first line of 2 Thessalonians 2 actually disproves popular ideas. Paul wrote about "the coming of our Lord Jesus Christ" and "our gathering together unto him" (2:1). "Our gathering" clearly refers to the Rapture of the Church. But when does this gathering take place? At the coming of our Lord Jesus Christ. What Greek word does Paul use here for "coming"? *Parousia!* This exact same word is also used in verse 8 which speaks of the "brightness of *his coming* ['parousia']." A simple comparison of verse 1 with verse 8 proves two things beyond question: (1)

"Parousia" refers to the visibly "bright" and ultra-glorious Second Coming of Jesus Christ (as in Matthew 24:27, 30, 31); (2) It is at this bright and highly visible Second Coming that Jesus Christ will gather His Church!

After referring to the "coming" or "parousia" of our Lord Jesus Christ, and our "gathering together to him," Paul solemnly warned, "Let no man deceive you by any means, for that day shall not come except there come *a falling away first,* and that man of sin be revealed, the son of perdition" (2 Thessalonians 2:3, 4). These words are so power-packed! Here are the fast facts:

(1) This is about the Antichrist.
(2) The Antichrist will rise as a result of "a falling away." The Greek word for "falling away" is "apostasia," from which we get the English word "apostasy," which means *a falling away from grace and truth inside the church!*
(3) This apostasy, resulting in the rise of the Antichrist, must come "first," that is, *before* "our gathering" to Jesus Christ. *Thus the Antichrist definitely comes before the Rapture!*
(4) It is Christians themselves who are in danger of being deceived about this, for Paul warned, "Let no man deceive *you* by any means."
(5) Antichrist is "the son of perdition," which is a phrase Jesus applied to Judas in John 17:12. Judas was a professed Christian within the inner circle of Christ's followers. Thus the Antichrist will not be someone like Nicolae

Carpathia, but will be *a professed follower of Jesus Christ!* Judas even kissed Jesus, saying, "Hail, master" (Matthew 26:49), yet it was a kiss of betrayal.

(6) The Antichrist is called *"that* man of sin," which is the same as the little horn which had "eyes *like* the eyes of a man" (Daniel 7:8). Daniel did not say the horn would *be* only one man, but that it would have "eyes *like* the eyes of a man." This is a subtle, and yet highly significant difference.

Continuing his description of the Antichrist, Paul wrote, "Who opposeth and exalteth himself above all that is called God, or that is worshipped; so that he as God sitteth in the temple of God, shewing himself that he is God" (2 Thessalonians 2:4). Many apply this to a Nicolae Carpathia-type of Antichrist whom they think will someday enter a rebuilt Jewish temple, sit down, and boldly proclaim, "I am God;" yet is this what Paul is really saying? If you look at any concordance, you will discover that the Greek word used here for "temple" is "naos." Paul used the very same word in 1 Corinthians. Writing to "the church of God" (1:2), Paul asked, "Know ye not that *ye are the temple of God"* (3:16, emphasis added)? Here the temple of God is *the church,* and Paul wrote that this is where the Antichrist will sit! This doesn't mean that the Antichrist will literally sit down on some chair inside a physical building. To "sit" means to sit in a position of supreme authority. Jesus is now "seated" at the right hand of God. The Antichrist will "sit" in God's temple, which means he will sit in a position of supreme and apparently infallible authority *inside* the Christian Church. Thus the Antichrist will direct the eyes of people to himself in the place of Jesus Christ. Thus the battle is between "that man of sin" and "the Man Christ Jesus." And this Antichrist will not blatantly *say,* "I am God," for this would be much too obvious and non-seductive. Rather, the Antichrist will sit *"as* God…*shewing himself* that he is God" (2:4, emphasis added) by his statements and claims.

The Antichrist will sit in "the temple of God." Millions are now applying this to a rebuilt temple in Jerusalem, and this is one reason why American Christians are so interested in the latest news about the Israelis and the Palestinian Liberation Organization. Yet think about it. If certain Jews ever do rebuild their temple and start offering sacrifices, would this temple really be "the temple *of God"?* When Jesus Christ died, He "caused the sacrifice…to cease" (Daniel 9:27). He was the Final Sacrifice. If the Jews ever do resume animal sacrifices, what kind of statement would this be making to the Father? It would be an official denial of His Son! Therefore (are you ready for this?) that temple would itself be an *antichrist temple!* Honestly, could such a temple, which would in itself be a denial of Jesus, ever be properly called "the temple *of God"?* Never! (For more information on this subject, see my other book, *Exploding the Israel Deception,* Chapter 8, "Titanic Truths about the Temple.")

Paul told the Thessalonians, "And you know

what withholdeth, that he might be revealed in his time" (2 Thessalonians 2:6. Note: "withholdeth" here means "restrains" in modern English. See the New King James translation of this verse). Another extremely controversial issue is, "Who or what is the restrainer which holds back the Antichrist?" Many popular Bible teachers believe the "restrainer" is the Holy Spirit inside the Christian Church. This theory says that as long as the Church remains in this world, the Antichrist cannot come. Only after the church is "taken out of the way" (verse 7) in the Rapture can Antichrist appear. Yet think about it. If the Holy Spirit is removed with the Church at the Rapture, how could there ever be a Tribulation Force of new believers? For there would be no Holy Spirit left on earth to convert them! And if somehow the Holy Spirit is still in this world after the Rapture, wouldn't He then be dwelling in the Tribulation Force? He would have to be, because the Bible says no man can resist Antichrist without the Holy Spirit dwelling *inside* of him (1 John 4:4, 5). So, why wouldn't the Holy Spirit dwelling inside the Tribulation Force after the Rapture restrain the Antichrist? Why could the Holy Spirit inside a Pre-Tribulation Church restrain him, yet the Holy Spirit inside a Post-Tribulation Church could not? *Friend, there is something wrong with this picture!*

Paul continued his description of the Antichrist when he wrote, "The mystery of iniquity doth already work" (2:7). According to these words, the Antichrist was "already" at work in Paul's day. Verse 8 says, "And then shall that Wicked be revealed, whom the Lord shall consume with the spirit of his mouth and shall destroy with the brightness of his coming ['parousia']." Thus the Antichrist will continue until the visible return of Jesus Christ. A simple combining of verse 7 with verse 8 reveals that the Antichrist *started* in the time of Paul and *continues* to the end, which makes it *impossible* for the Antichrist to be only one man! Not only that, it is at the bright and visible return of Jesus, at the "parousia" (verses 8), *when* Christ will destroy the Antichrist and "gather" His Church (verse 1). This makes it *impossible* for the Church to be the "restrainer!"

Then who is the "restrainer"? We must put Paul's words under a microscope to catch the right clues. Paul told the Thessalonians, "Remember ye not, that when I was yet with you *I told you* these things? And now *ye know* what withholdeth…" (2 Thessalonians 2:5, 6, emphasis added). Do you see it? The early Church did "know" who the "withholder" or "restrainer" was, for Paul plainly says he had told them. Therefore, in order for us to know who the "restrainer" is, we must *go back* into ancient history and find out what the early Church actually said about this subject, rather than looking to modern interpreters. When we do this, the answer becomes very clear.

H. Grattan Guinness, who has been called England's greatest teacher of prophecy, wrote: "The early church tells us what it did know about the subject, and no one in these days can be in a position to contradict its testimony as to what Paul had, by word of mouth only, told the Thessalonians. It is a point on which ancient tradition alone *can* have any authority. Modern speculation is positively impertinent on such a subject....From *Irenaeus,* who lived close to apostolic times, down to *Chrysostom* and *Jerome,* the Fathers taught that the power withholding the manifestation of the 'man of sin' was *the Roman Empire as governed by the Caesars....*While the Caesars held imperial power, it was impossible for the predicted antichrist to arise, and that on the fall of the Caesars he *would* arise" (*Romanism and the Reformation,* pp. 105–107. Italics original). Thus the early Church believed the "restrainer" *was the Roman Empire ruled by the Caesars.*

Why didn't Paul just come right out and tell us this in his letter? Wouldn't that have solved a lot of problems? Actually, there is a good reason why he didn't. The Thessalonians were already going though "persecutions" from the Roman Empire (1 Thessalonians 1:4). If this letter had specified that the Roman Empire would someday be "taken out of the way," this might have caused even more problems for those early believers. What if this letter fell into the wrong hands? If the Roman authorities discovered that these Christians believed the Roman Empire would eventually fall, they would have considered this high treason against Caesar! Again the cry would ring out, "To the Coliseum with the Christians!" So, in order to protect them, Paul told them privately without writing it down.

In his book *Champions of Christianity*, Ralph Thompson wrote, "Paul did not identify the *restraining power* which they knew to be Rome, for fear of reprisals. Remember the Christian church was under persecution by Rome. If the Thessalonian Christians were aware of Daniel seven, showing the rise of the 'little horn' after the fourth kingdom of Rome (see Daniel 7:8, 24), then the *restraining power of Rome* against the revelation of the *Great Apostasy* of the Christian Church made sense" (*Champions of Christianity in Search of Truth,* by Ralph Thompson, Teach Services, Inc. Brushton, New York. 1996. p. 47. Italics original). When the early Church Fathers wrote about the "restrainer," they used the secret code words of Scripture: *"The 'restrainer' is the fourth beast of Daniel 7,"* which they knew was the Roman Empire. This is what Paul whispered when he "told them," and this fits the prophecy perfectly. Daniel 7 predicted that after the fourth beast fell, *then* the little horn would appear, and historically, that's what happened. When the Caesars went down, the Popes came up to full power, and the Antichrist was revealed.

Martin Luther, John Calvin, and John Wesley, along with countless others, all believed "that man of sin," described in 2 Thessalonians 2:3, applied to the Papal office of "the pope, sitting as God in the temple of God" (J. H. Merle d'Aubingne, *History of the Reformation of the Sixteenth Century,* Book I, Ch. III, p. 17). Martin Luther "proved, by the revelations of Daniel and St. John, *by the epistles of Paul,* and St. Jude, that the reign of Antichrist, predicted and described in the Bible, was the Papacy" (d'Aubingne, Book XIII, Ch. VI, p. 520. Italics supplied). As with the prophecy of Daniel 7, all of the major Protestant Reformers interpreted Paul's prophecy in 2 Thessalonians 2 to be historical, chronological, and successive, with NO GAPS.

The Westminster Confession of Faith (1647), ratified and established by an act of the British Parliament, declares: "There is no other head of the Church but the Lord Jesus Christ: nor can the Pope of Rome, in any sense be head thereof; but is that Antichrist, that man of sin and son of perdition, that exalteth himself in the church against Christ, and all that is called God" (Phillip Schaff, *The Creeds of Christendom, With a History and Critical Notes.* New York: Harper & Brothers, 1919, vol. III, chap. 25. sec. 6. p. 658, 659). It is only fair to say that Rome is not alone in its problem of self-exaltation above Jesus Christ. This was Lucifer's original sin, and every true Christian also struggles with this. Catholics, Protestants, Evangelicals, Muslims, Jews, and Steve Wohlberg, all need to gain the victory over pride *through the grace of God.* When it comes to basic human sin, we are all in this together.

Here's a simple summary of 2 Thessalonians 2: In Paul's own day, the "mystery of iniquity" was already at work (2:7). The "falling away" had begun, and "that man of sin" was beginning to rise. But the Roman Empire with its Caesars was yet "restraining" the Antichrist's rise to full power. In 476 A.D., when imperial Rome fell, being "taken out of the way," the Popes rose up as the main power-brokers of Europe, and the Antichrist was revealed. The Antichrist will continue until the end of the world. Then Jesus Christ will return with the "brightness of his coming," destroy the Antichrist, and gather His Church to Himself. Who might belong to that Church? In light of the context, it must be those who have *not fallen away from the truth!* Like the crackling of thunder, the voice of Paul cries out to us in the 21st century: "Let no man deceive you by any means"! The above interpretation is the only one that fully agrees with what Paul wrote and with what the early Church actually said.

Off the coast of Florida, between Cuba and the Bermuda Islands, exists a stretch of ocean called the Bermuda Triangle. Many ships have mysteriously vanished in those waters. No one knows why. When it comes to Bible prophecy, the ancient Protestant understanding of *who the Beast is* has also largely vanished into the waves of history. Does anyone know why?

Yes, many do, and in our next chapter you will join their ranks.

Then you will know *why* truth has been left behind.

Chapter 3
The Evil Empire of Jesuit Futurism

Imagine a pair of supernatural, high-tech, Heaven-inspired eyeglasses that can give a Christian the instant ability to *see* one of Lucifer's greatest end-time deceptions. Such X-ray eyeglasses do exist. The purpose of this chapter is help you find them and put them on, and then you will be able to understand the almost unimaginable Evil Empire of *Jesuit Futurism*.

Modern Christianity has largely forgotten the importance of the Protestant Reformation, which took place during the 1500s. "The sixteenth century presents the spectacle of a stormy sunrise after a dismal night. Europe awoke from long sleep of superstition. The dead arose. The witnesses to truth who had been silenced and slain stood up once more and renewed their testimony. The martyred confessors reappeared in the Reformers. There was a cleansing of the spiritual sanctuary. Civil and religious liberty were inaugurated. The discovery of printing and revival of learning accelerated the movement. There was progress everywhere. Columbus struck across the ocean and opened a new hemisphere to view. Rome was shaken on her seven hills, and lost one-half of her dominions. Protestant nations were created. The modern world was called into existence" (H. Grattan Guinness, *Romanism and the Reformation,* p. 122).

For almost a thousand years, Europe had been ruled by the iron hand of Rome. Only a few Bibles existed then, and Christianity was largely permeated with superstition. Faith in Jesus Christ, heartfelt appreciation for His love, and a simple trust in His death on the cross, were almost unknown. The New Testament truth about grace, full forgiveness, and the free gift of eternal life to believers in the Son of God (Romans 6:23), had been buried under a mass of tradition. Then Martin Luther arose like a lion in Germany. After a period of tremendous personal struggle, Martin Luther began teaching justification by faith in Jesus Christ (being declared "just" by God), rather than through reliance on "creature merits," or any human works (Romans 1:16; 3:26, 28; 5:1).

Eventually, Martin Luther turned to the prophecies. By candlelight, he read about the "little horn," the "man of sin," and "the beast," and he was shocked as the Holy Spirit spoke to his heart. Finally, he saw the truth and said to himself, "Why, these prophecies apply to the Roman Catholic Church!" As he wrestled with this new insight, the voice of God echoed loudly in his soul, saying, "Preach the word!" (2 Timothy 4:2). And so, at the risk of losing his life, Martin Luther preached publicly and in print to an astonished people that Papal Rome was indeed the Antichrist of Bible prophecy. Because of this dual message of salvation through faith in Jesus Christ apart from works *and* of Papal Rome being the Antichrist, the river of history literally changed its course. Hundreds of thousands of people in Europe and in England left the Catholic Church.

"'There are two great truths that stand out in the preaching that brought about the Protestant Reformation,' American Bible Commentator, Ralph Woodrow, reminds us, 'The just shall live by faith, not by the works of Romanism and the Papacy is the Antichrist of Scripture.' It was a message for Christ and against Antichrist. The entire Reformation rests upon this twofold testimony'" (Michael de Semlyen, *All Roads Lead to Rome,* Dorchester House Publications, Dorchester House, England, 1991, pp. 202, 203). It has been said that the Reformation first discovered Jesus Christ, and then, in the blazing light of Christ, *it discovered the Antichrist.* This mighty, Spirit-filled movement, *for* Christ and *against* the Antichrist, shook the world.

H. Grattan Guinness wrote these memorable words: "From the first, and throughout, that movement [the Reformation] was energized and guided by the prophetic word. *Luther* never felt strong and free to war against the Papal apostasy till he recognized the pope as antichrist. It was then that he burned the Papal bull. *Knox's* first sermon, the sermon that launched him on his mission as a reformer, was on the prophecies concerning the Papacy. The reformers embodied their interpretations of prophecy in their confessions of faith, and Calvin in his 'Institutes.' All of the reformers were *unanimous* in the matter, even the mild and cautious Melanchthon was as assured of the antipapal meaning of these prophecies as was Luther himself. And their interpretation of these prophecies determined their reforming action. It led them to protest against Rome with extraordinary strength and undaunted courage. It nerved them to resist the claims of the apostate Church to the utmost. It made them martyrs; it sustained them at the stake. And the views of the Reformers were shared by thousands, by hundreds of thousands. They were adopted by princes and peoples. Under their influence nations abjured their allegiance to the false priest of Rome. In the reaction that followed, all the powers of hell seemed to be let loose upon the adherents of the Reformation. War followed war: tortures, burnings, and massacres were multiplied. Yet the Reformation stood undefeated and unconquerable. God's word upheld it, and the energies of His Almighty Spirit. It was the work of Christ as truly as the founding of the Church eighteen centuries ago; and the revelation of the future which he gave from heaven — that prophetic book with which the Scripture closes — was one of the mightiest instruments employed in its accomplishment " (H. Grattan Guinness, *Romanism and the Reformation,* pp. 136, 137).

In 1545, the Catholic Church convened one of its most famous councils in history, which took place north of Rome in a city called Trent. The Council of Trent actually continued for three sessions, ending in 1563. One of the main purposes of this Council was for Catholics to plan a counterattack against Martin Luther and the Protestants. Thus the Council of Trent became a center for Rome's Counter-Reformation. Up to this point, Rome's main method of attack had been largely frontal — the open burning of Bibles and of heretics. Yet this warfare only *confirmed* in the minds of Protestants the conviction that Papal Rome was indeed the Beast which would "make war with the saints" (Revelation 13:7). Therefore a new tactic was needed, something less obvious. *This is where the Jesuits come in.*

On August 15, 1534, Ignatius Loyola founded a secret Catholic order called the Society of Jesus, also known as the Jesuits. Historically, we might compare this order to Darth Vader's Evil Empire in the classic Star Wars films. The Jesuits definitely have a dark history of intrigue and sedition, that's why they were expelled from Portugal (1759), France (1764), Spain (1767), Naples (1767), and Russia (1820). "Jesuit priests have been known throughout history as the most wicked political arm of the Roman Catholic Church. Edmond Paris, in his scholarly work, *The Secret History of the Jesuits,* reveals and documents much of this information" (*Seventy Weeks: The Historical Alternative,* by Robert Caringola. Abundant Life Ministries Reformed Press, 1991, p. 31). At the Council of Trent, the Catholic Church gave the Jesuits *the specific assignment of destroying Protestantism* and bringing people back to the Mother Church. This was to be done not only through the Inquisition and through torture, *but also through theology.*

It's time to discover those X-ray eyeglasses. At the Council of Trent, the Jesuits were commissioned by the Pope to develop a new interpretation of Scripture that would counteract the Protestant application of the Bible's antichrist prophecies to the Roman Catholic Church. Francisco Ribera (1537–1591), a brilliant Jesuit priest and doctor of theology from Spain, basically said, "Here am I, send me." Like Martin Luther, Francisco Ribera also read by candlelight the prophecies about the Antichrist, the little horn, that man of sin, and the Beast. But because the Pope was his boss, he came to conclusions vastly different from those of the Protestants. "Why, these prophecies don't apply to the Catholic Church at all!" Ribera said. Then to whom do they apply? Ribera proclaimed, "To only one sinister man who will rise up at the end of time!" "Fantastic!" was the reply from Rome, and this viewpoint was quickly adopted as the official Roman Catholic position on the Antichrist.

"In 1590, Ribera published a commentary on the Revelation as a counter-interpretation to the prevailing view among Protestants which identified the Papacy with the Antichrist. Ribera applied all the book of Revelation but the earliest chapters to the end time rather than to the history of the Church. Antichrist would be *a single evil person* who would be received by the Jews and would rebuild Jerusalem" (George Eldon Ladd, *The Blessed Hope: A Biblical Study of the Second Advent and the Rapture.* Grand Rapids, MI: Eerdmans, 1956, pp. 37–38). "Ribera denied the Protestant Scriptural Antichrist (2 Thessalonians 2) as seated in the church of God — asserted by Augustine, Jerome, Luther and many reformers. He set on an *infidel Antichrist, outside the church of God.*" (Ralph Thompson, *Champions of Christianity in Search of Truth,* p. 89). "The result of his work [Ribera's] was a twisting and maligning of prophetic truth" (Robert Caringola, *Seventy Weeks: The Historical Alternative*, p. 32).

Following close behind Francisco Ribera was another brilliant Jesuit scholar, Cardinal Robert Bellarmine (1542–1621) of Rome. Between 1581 and 1593, Cardinal Bellarmine published his "Polemic Lectures Concerning the Disputed Points of the Christian Belief Against the Heretics of this Time." In these lectures, he agreed with Ribera. "The futurist teachings of Ribera were further popularized by an Italian cardinal and the most renowned of all Jesuit controversialists. His writings claimed that Paul, Daniel, and John had nothing whatsoever to say about the Papal power. The futurists' school won general acceptance among Catholics. They were taught that antichrist was a single individual who would not rule until the very end of time" (*Great Prophecies of the Bible,* by Ralph Woodrow, p. 198). Through the work of these two tricky Jesuit scholars, we might say that *a brand new baby was born into the world.* Protestant historians have given this baby a name — *Jesuit Futurism.* In fact, Francisco Ribera has been called the Father of Futurism.

Before we go much farther, let's define some terms. *Historicism* is the belief that Biblical prophecies about the little horn, the man of sin, the Antichrist, the Beast, and the Babylonian Harlot of Revelation 17, all apply to *the developing history of Christianity and to the ongoing struggle between Jesus Christ and Satan within the Christian Church,* culminating at the end of time. Historicism sees these prophecies as having a direct application to Papal Rome *as a system* whose doctrines are actually a denial of the New Testament message of free salvation by grace through simple faith in Jesus Christ, apart from works. Historicism was the primary prophetic viewpoint of the Protestant Reformers. In direct opposition to Historicism, and rising up as a razor-sharp counter-attack on Protestantism, was the Evil Empire of the Jesuits with their viewpoint of *Futurism,* which basically says, "The Antichrist prophecies have nothing to do with the history of Papal Rome, rather, they apply to *only one sinister man* who comes at the end."

Thus Jesuit Futurism sweeps 1,500 years of prophetic history under the proverbial rug by inserting its infamous GAP. The GAP theory teaches that when Rome fell, prophecy stopped, only to continue again right around the time of the Rapture. Thus the ten horns, the little horn, the Beast, and the Antichrist *have nothing to do with Christians today.*

According to this viewpoint, how many prophecies were being fulfilled during the Dark Ages? None. Zero.

For almost 300 years after the Council of Trent, this Catholic baby (Jesuit Futurism) remained largely inside the crib of Catholicism, but the plan of the Jesuits was that this baby would grow up and *finally be adopted by Protestants*. This adoption process actually began in the early 1800s in England, and from there it spread to America. The story of how this happened is both fascinating and tragic. As I briefly share some of the highlights, I want to clarify that many of those whom I will mention were (and are) genuine Christians. But is it possible for a Christian to unknowingly become a channel for error? In other words, can a sincere Christian be used by both Jesus Christ *and* the devil? At first we might say, "Never!" but consider this. In Matthew 16, Jesus told Peter that God was blessing him as he shared his faith in Christ (16:15–17), and then, just a few minutes later, Peter yielded to temptation and Satan spoke through him (16:21–23)! This proves that a Christian *can* be used by both God and Lucifer, and all within a short space of time. I call this the *Peter Principle.*

"The Futurism of Ribera never posed a positive threat to the Protestants for three centuries. It was virtually confined to the Roman Church. But early in the nineteenth century it sprang forth with vehemence and latched on to Protestants of the Established Church of England" (Ralph Thompson, *Champions of Christianity in Search of Truth,* p. 91). Dr. Samuel Roffey Maitland (1792–1866), a lawyer and Bible scholar, became a librarian to the Archbishop of Canterbury. It is very likely that one day he discovered Ribera's commentary in the library. In any event, in 1826 he published a widely-read book attacking the Reformation and supporting Ribera's idea of a future one-man Antichrist. For the next ten years, in tract after tract, he continued his anti-Reformation rhetoric. As a result of his zeal and strong attacks against the Reformation in England, the Protestantism of that very nation which produced the *King James Bible* (1611) received a crushing blow.

After Dr. Maitland came James H. Todd, a professor of Hebrew at the University of Dublin. Todd accepted the futuristic ideas of Maitland, publishing his own supportive pamphlets and books. Then came John Henry Newman (1801–1890), a member of the Church of England and a leader of the famous Oxford Movement (1833–1845). In 1850, Newman wrote his "Letter on Anglican Difficulties" revealing that one of the goals in the Oxford Movement was to finally absorb "the various English denominations and parties" back into the Church of Rome. After publishing a pamphlet endorsing Todd's futurism about a one-man Antichrist, Newman soon became a full Roman Catholic, and later even a highly honored Cardinal. Through the influence of Maitland, Todd, Newman, and others, a definite "Romeward movement was already arising, destined to sweep away the old Protestant landmarks, as with a flood" (H. Grattan Guinness, *History Unveiling Prophecy or Time as an Interpreter,* New York:

Fleming H. Revell Co., 1905, p. 289).

Then came the much-respected Scottish Presbyterian minister Edward Irving (1792–1834), the acknowledged forerunner of both the Pentecostal and Charismatic Movements. Irving pastored the large Chalcedonian Chapel in London with over 1,000 members. When Irving turned to the prophecies, he eventually accepted the one-man Antichrist idea of Todd, Maitland, Bellarmine, and Ribera, yet he went a step further. Somewhere around 1830, Edward Irving began to teach the unique idea of a two-phase return of Christ, *the first phase being a secret rapture prior to the rise of the Antichrist.* Where he got this idea is a matter of much dispute. Journalist Dave MacPherson believes Irving accepted it is a result of a prophetic revelation given to a young Scottish girl named Margaret McDonald (*The Incredible Cover-Up: Exposing the Origins of Rapture Theories*, by Dave MacPherson. Omega Publications, Medford Oregon. 1980). In any case, the fact is, Irving *taught it!*

In the midst of this growing anti-Protestant climate in England, there arose a man by the name of John Nelson Darby (1800–1882). A brilliant lawyer, pastor, and theologian, he wrote more than 53 books on Bible subjects. A much-respected Christian and a man of deep piety, Darby took a strong stand in favor of the infallibility of the Bible in contrast with the liberalism of his day. He became one of the leaders of a group in Plymouth, England, which became known as the Plymouth Brethren. Darby's contribution to the development of evangelical theology has been so great that he has been called The Father of Modern Dispensationalism. Yet John Nelson Darby, like Edward Irving, also became a strong promoter of a Pre-Tribulation Rapture followed by a one-man Antichrist. In fact, this teaching has become a hallmark of Dispensationalism.

Dispensationalism is the theory that God deals with mankind in major dispensations or periods. According to Darby, we are now in the "Church Age," that is, until the Rapture. After the Rapture, then the seven-year period of Daniel 9:27 will supposedly kick in, and this is when the Antichrist will rise up against the Jews. In fact, John Nelson Darby laid much of the foundation for the present popular removal of Daniel's 70th week away from history and from Jesus Christ in favor of applying it to a future Tribulation after the Rapture. Thus, in spite of all the positives of his ministry, Darby followed Maitland, Todd, Bellarmine, and Ribera *by incorporating the teachings of counter-reformation Futurism into his theology.* This created a link between John Nelson Darby, the Father of Dispensationalism, and the Jesuit Francisco Ribera, the Father of Futurism. Darby visited America six times between 1859–1874, preaching in all of its major cities, during which time he definitely planted the seeds of Futurism in American soil. The child of the Jesuits was growing up.

One of the most important figures in this whole drama is Cyris Ingerson Scofield (1843–1921), a Kansas lawyer who was greatly influenced by the writings of Darby. In 1909, Scofield published the first edition of his famous *Scofield Reference Bible*. In the early 1900s, this Bible became so popular in American Protestant Bible Schools that it was necessary to print literally millions of copies. Yet, in the much-respected footnotes of this very Bible, Scofield injected large doses of the fluid of Futurism also found in the writings of Darby, Todd, Maitland, Bellarmine, and Ribera. Through the *Scofield Bible*, the Jesuit child reached young adulthood. The doctrine of an Antichrist *still to come* was becoming firmly established inside 20th-century American Protestantism.

The Moody Bible Institute and the Dallas Theological Seminary have strongly supported the teachings of John Nelson Darby, and this has continued to fuel Futurism's growth. Then in the 1970s, Pastor Hal Lindsey, a graduate of Dallas Theological Seminary, released his blockbuster book *The Late Great Planet Earth*. This 177-page, easy-to-read volume brought Futurism to the masses of American Christianity, and beyond. The *New York Times* labeled it "The number one best-seller of the decade." Over 30 million copies have been sold, and it has been translated into over 30 languages. Through *The Late Great Planet Earth*, the child of Jesuit Futurism became a man.

Then came *Left Behind*. In the 1990s, Tim LaHaye and Jerry Jenkins (writer-in-residence at the Moody Bible Institute) took the future one-man Antichrist idea of Hal Lindsey, Scofield, Darby, Irving, Newman, Todd, Maitland, Bellarmine, and Ribera, and turned it into "The most successful

Christian-fiction series ever" *(Publishers Weekly)*. Hal Lindsey's book, *The Late Great Planet Earth,* was largely theological, which limited its appeal, while *Left Behind* is a sequence of highly imaginative novels, "overflowing with suspense, action, and adventure," a "Christian thriller," with a "label its creators could never have predicted: blockbuster success" *(Entertainment Weekly)*. The much-respected television ministries of Jack Van Impe, Peter and Paul Lalonde, and Pastor John Hagee, have all worked together to produce *LEFT BEHIND: The Movie.* The books have reached the best-seller lists of the *New York Times* and the *Wall Street Journal,* resulting in an interview of LaHaye and Jenkins on *Larry King Live.* The *Left Behind* books have been made available on displays at Wal-Mart, Fry's Electronics, Costco, and inside countless other stores.

Again let me clarify. I believe the authors of *Left Behind* and the leaders of these television ministries are genuine Christians who are doing their best to influence people for the Kingdom. God is using them, just like the Father spoke through Peter when he firmly confessed his faith in Christ (Matthew 16:15–17). Remember that Peter Principle. There is much that is good in *Left Behind* which God can use to influence people for Jesus Christ. But, in the full light of Scripture, prophecy, and the Protestant Reformation, something is terribly wrong. *Left Behind* is now teaching much of the very same Jesuit Futurism of Francisco Ribera which is *hiding the real truth about the Antichrist.* Through *Left Behind,* the floodgates of Futurism have been opened, unleashing a massive tidal wave of false prophecy that is now sweeping over America. Sadly, it is a false "idea whose time has come."

As we have already seen, the theological *foundation* for the entire *Left Behind* series is the application of the "seven years" of Daniel 9:27 to a future period of Tribulation. Are you ready for this? Guess who was one of the very first scholars to slice Daniel's 70th week away from the first 69 weeks, sliding it down to the end of time? It was the Evil Empire's very own Francisco Ribera! "Ribera's primary apparatus was the seventy weeks. He taught that Daniel's 70th week was still in the future....It was as though God put a giant rubber band on this Messianic time measure. Does this supposition sound familiar? This is exactly the scenario used by Hal Lindsey and a multitude of other current prophecy teachers" (Robert Caringola, *Seventy Weeks: The Historical Alternative*, p. 35).

When most Christians look at the last 1,500 years, how much fulfilled prophecy do they see? None, zero, because almost everything is now being applied to a future time period after the Rapture. As we have seen, this GAP idea originated with the Jesuits, and its insertion into the majority of 21st century prophetic teaching is now blinding millions of hearts and eyes to what has gone before, and to what is happening *right now inside the Church.* "It is this GAP theory that permeates Futurism's interpretation of all apocalyptic prophecy" (Ralph Thompson, *Champions of Christianity in Search of Truth,* p. 90). In love and in the Spirit of Jesus Christ, someone should publicly appeal to the major prophetic television ministries of today to re-evaluate their positions. Hopefully, like noble ships with a new command from their captain, they will yet change their course.

Jesuit Futurism has now become like a giant, seven-foot, 400-pound boxer, with spiked gloves. With a seemingly all-powerful punch, it has almost knocked Protestant Historicism entirely out of the ring. "The proper eschatological term for the view most taught today is *Futurism*...which fuels the confusion of *Dispensationalism*. The futuristic school of Bible prophecy came from the Roman Catholic Church, specifically her Jesuit theologians....However the alternative has been believed for centuries. It is known as *Historicism*" (Robert Caringola, *Seventy Weeks: The Historical Alternative,* p. 6). "It is a matter for deep regret that those who hold and advocate the Futurist system at the present day, Protestants as they are for the most part, are thus really playing into the hands of Rome, and helping to screen the Papacy from detection as the Antichrist" (*Daniel and the Revelation: The Chart of Prophecy and Our Place In It, A Study of the Historical and Futurist Interpretation,* by Joseph Tanner, London: Hodder and Stoughton, 1898, p. 16).

Who had the right theology — those who were burned at the stake for Jesus Christ, or those who lit the fires? Who had the true Bible doctrine — the martyrs or their persecutors? Who had the correct interpretation of the Antichrist — those who died trusting in the blood of Christ, or those who shed the blood of God's dear saints? Dear friend, the Evil

Empire of Jesuit Futurism is now *at war* with the Protestant Reformation by denying its power-packed application of prophecy to the Vatican. "The futurist school of Bible prophecy was created for one reason, and one reason only: to counter the Protestant Reformation!" (Robert Caringola, *Seventy Weeks: The Historical Alterative*, p. 34). In fact, this Evil Empire of Jesuit Futurism is at war with the prophecies of the Word of God itself! And if that's not enough, consider this. Jesuit Futurism originated with the Roman Catholic Church, which makes it *the very doctrine of the Antichrist!* And when Christian ministries and movies like *A Thief in the Night, Apocalypse, Revelation, Tribulation,* and *Left Behind,* proclaim an Antichrist who comes only after the Rapture, what are they really doing? I shudder to even say it. Are you ready for this? They are sincerely and yet unknowingly *teaching the doctrine of the Antichrist!*

You have discovered those heavenly X-ray eyeglasses. You are now able to see *The Left Behind Deception.*

I appeal to you in the loving name of Jesus Christ, the Crucified One — *Don't fall for it!*

Special Note

(1) *The Left Behind Deception* is a smaller version of a larger book called *Truth Left Behind*, which has 9 chapters and 192 pages. The bigger book, *Truth Left Behind*, picks up where *The Left Behind Deception* leaves off, contains "the rest of the story," and includes more exciting information about the love of Jesus Christ, the Protestant Reformation, the United States of America, the Image of the Beast, the Mark of the Beast, and Earth's final days.

See next page for details! ☞

(2) This little book, *The Left Behind Deception* is great for sharing! A large discount is available when quantities of 100 books or more are purchased for mass distribution. To order additional copies, call 1-800-795-7171.

(Visa / MasterCard Accepted)

For more information please go to the website at
www.truthleftbehind.com.

Don't miss the grand finale!

Truth Left Behind continues a thoughtful analysis of Time LaHaye and Jerry Jenkins best-selling *Left Behind* series, revealing even more misunderstood secrets about Earth's last days. Power-packed chapters include: The Return of the Wounded Beast, America in Bible Prophecy, Talking Statues and the Image of the Beast, Microsoft and the Mark of the Beast, New Babylon and the Shepherd's Call, The Flames of the Martyrs Still Speak.

What about Israel in Bible prophecy?

The *Left Behind* novels describe a rebuilt Jewish Temple and point toward a fiery Middle East battle called Armageddon. Book Six declares; "World history and prophecy collide in Jerusalem at the middle of the Tribulation for the most explosive episode yet of the continuing drama of those left behind" *(Assassins,* inside cover). Does the Book of Revelation really focus on the Middle East, or has *more truth been left behind?*

To Order Now Call
1-800-795-7171
Visa / MasterCard Accepted!